The Reflective Advantage

*Achieving Dynamic Leadership
Excellence Through Listening*

By
R. Harrison Baxter

DEDICATION

Dedicated to all current and future CEO'S, entrepreneurs, managers and thought leaders who embody the art of reflective listening, fostering environments of empathy, growth, and collaboration. Your commitment to understanding others' perspectives paves the way for meaningful change and collective progress. May this book inspire you to continue nurturing inclusive and thriving communities, guided by the principles of empathy and respect.

TABLE OF CONTENTS

INTRODUCTION

Every successful business and every successful relationship require strong leadership. Rapid and critical changes in the industry and the private sector in recent years have led to a loss of traditional leadership and effective relationship strategies and a reduced focus on actively listening to and interpreting the perspectives of others. Simply put, we don't listen to each other anymore. This has led to increasing numbers of professional and personal divorces, while business and personal relationships are not valued or respected as they used to be.

Successful leaders must articulate their vision and mission effectively and recognize and identify the contributions of others. People must be inspired, motivated, and open to criticism and constructive feedback. Leaders must stay current with the latest trends and technologies to compete in the market.

Leadership is an ongoing process, and to be successful, leaders must be proactive in embracing change and adapting to new ways of leading. Listening to the ideas and feedback of others enables leaders to make more informed decisions and create a better working environment. This produces an environment where employees can develop and grow personally and relationally, allowing everyone to reach their full potential.

The need for more active leadership strategies has become increasingly important in the modern world, and prevention-based leadership is emerging as a more practical approach. This book will explore the critical elements of prevention-based leadership and discuss how it differs from other leadership styles. We will look at different ways to implement solution-based leadership and discuss the benefits.

Critical features of prevention-based leadership include a focus on prompt action, anticipating and planning for potential disasters, and taking action to prevent escalation of situations as leaders can identify potential risks and develop strategies to deal with them. They can also adjust their plans as needed, taking proactive measures to ensure their team's success.

Prevention-based Leadership has many advantages. It encourages collaboration and team building and helps create an environment where everyone works together to achieve their goals. It also helps keep costs down, as preventive measures are generally less expensive than proactive measures. It helps keep workers and customers safe, as preventative measures can help avoid dangerous situations. It also anticipates problems and can reveal potential solutions before it is too late.

This book will explore prevention-based leadership in more detail and discuss how it differs from other leadership styles. We will examine the critical elements of preventive leadership and its benefits. By understanding the concept and its benefits, leaders can develop an effective prevention-based leadership style to help improve their team's performance

CHAPTER 1

WHAT IS PREVENTIVE BASED LEADERSHIP?

"True leadership is not solely defined by how one reacts to problems, but rather by how one prevents them from arising in the first place." –

John C. Maxwell.

Preventive-based leadership is a management approach that emphasizes proactive problem-solving to prevent potential issues from occurring rather than reacting to them after they have already happened. The method requires leaders to be forward-thinking, data-driven, and willing to invest resources in preventing potential issues. By implementing preventive-based leadership strategies, organizations can create a culture of continuous improvement and achieve better results over time. Preventive-based leadership aims to develop a culture of continuous improvement by identifying potential problems and taking proactive measures to prevent them from occurring.

Preventive-based leadership is based on the idea that it is more efficient and effective to prevent problems before they happen rather than dealing with the consequences after they occur. This approach requires leaders to be proactive and anticipate potential issues before they arise. Leaders must also be willing to take action to prevent those issues from occurring, even if it means investing resources or making changes to existing processes.

Preventive-based leadership is often associated with quality management systems, such as Six Sigma or Total Quality Management. These systems emphasize the importance of preventing defects and improving processes to achieve better results. Preventive-based leadership also requires a strong focus on data and analysis, as leaders must use data to identify potential problems and track the effectiveness of preventive measures. It involves several fundamental principles and strategies leaders can use to identify and prevent possible problems. These include:

1) Risk assessment: Leaders must assess the risks associated with their organization's products, services, and processes. This involves identifying potential hazards or failure points, analyzing the impact of those risks, and prioritizing actions to mitigate or eliminate them.

2) Proactive problem-solving: Leaders must take a proactive approach to problem-solving by anticipating potential issues and taking action to prevent them before they occur. This can involve redesigning products or processes, implementing new controls, or investing in new technologies or training programs.

3) Continuous improvement: Preventive-based leadership requires a culture of constant improvement, where leaders and employees are committed to identifying and addressing potential issues on an ongoing basis. This involves regularly reviewing and analyzing data to identify opportunities for improvement and implementing changes to processes, products, or services based on that analysis.

4) Data-driven decision-making: Leaders must use data to inform decisions and identify potential issues. This requires collecting and analyzing data regularly, using tools like statistical process control and root cause analysis to identify patterns and trends, and using that information to make data-driven decisions.

5) Employee empowerment: Leaders must empower employees to identify and address potential issues. This involves providing training and resources to employees, encouraging them to speak up about potential problems, and applying them in problem-solving.

6) Communication and collaboration: Preventive-based leadership requires effective communication and collaboration across all levels of the organization. Leaders must foster a culture of openness and transparency, encourage collaboration and knowledge sharing, and ensure that everyone in the organization is working towards the same goals.

How It Differs From Other Leadership Styles

Prevention Based Leadership is a very different concept. It involves making someone feel as if they are heard, building a relationship, perhaps a "highway" to someone's heart. Is the listener making the speaker comfortable about opening up? Are you listening or being a conversational narcissist? Here are five leadership styles and how each is compared to being a prevention-based leader.

1) **Reactive vs. Proactive**: Preventive-based leadership is a proactive management approach focused on preventing problems before they occur. For example, in a manufacturing setting, a preventive-based leader may implement a maintenance program to ensure equipment is regularly checked and maintained, reducing the risk of breakdowns or downtime (Hagen, 2018). In contrast, a reactive leader may only address equipment issues as they occur, resulting in lost production time and increased costs (Basu & Wright, 2018).

2) **Risk Management**: Preventive-based leadership strongly emphasizes risk management, identifying and mitigating potential risks before they become significant. For example, a preventive-based leader may conduct a risk assessment

to identify potential safety hazards in the workplace and take steps to mitigate those risks (Kaplan, 2018). In contrast, a laissez-faire leader may place less emphasis on risk management, leaving employees vulnerable to accidents or injuries.

3) **<u>Continuous Improvement</u>**: Preventive-based leadership emphasizes a culture of constant improvement, with leaders and employees working together to identify and address potential issues on an ongoing basis. For example, a preventive-based leader may use a process improvement framework like Six Sigma to identify and eliminate waste and inefficiencies in a process (Rath & Conchie, 2008). In contrast, a transactional leader may be more focused on maintaining the status quo and meeting current targets rather than actively seeking out opportunities for improvement.

4) **<u>Data-Driven Decision-Making</u>**: Preventive-based leadership relies heavily on data to inform decision-making, with leaders and employees using tools like statistical process control and root cause analysis to identify patterns and trends. For example, a preventive-based leader may use statistical process control to monitor key performance indicators and identify trends that could indicate potential issues (Montgomery, 2013). In contrast, a transformational leader may rely more on intuition and personal experience to make decisions.

5) **<u>Employee Empowerment</u>**: Preventive-based leadership empowers employees to identify and address potential issues, providing training and resources to help them do so. For example, a preventive-based leader may train employees in safety procedures and encourage them to report potential hazards (Burke et al., 2017). In contrast, an autocratic leader may be more hierarchical, with decision-making concentrated at the organization's top.

Preventive-based leaders focus on an organization's long-term success rather than short-term gains. These leaders take a holistic approach to problem-solving, identifying root causes, and implementing sustainable solutions. For example, a preventive-based leader may implement environmental management systems to reduce waste and emissions, focusing on creating a more sustainable business model (Eriksson & Kovalainen, 2015). This approach is consistent with the principles of sustainable business, which emphasize the importance of balancing economic, environmental, and social factors in decision-making. In contrast, transactional leaders may be more focused on achieving immediate results without considering the long-term implications of their actions.

Preventive-based leaders emphasize clear and proactive communication, with leaders and employees working to identify potential issues and develop solutions. For example, a preventive-based leader may use regular team meetings to discuss potential risks or opportunities, encouraging employees to speak up and share their ideas (McGonagle & Vella, 2018). In contrast, an authoritarian leader may be more focused on giving orders and expecting compliance without actively soliciting input from their team.

Preventive-based leaders emphasize a culture of continuous learning and improvement, with leaders and employees actively seeking opportunities for growth and development. In one such example, employees build new skills and stay up-to-date with industry trends (Stewart & Clarke, 2018). In contrast, a laissez-faire leader may focus less on employee development, leaving employees to fend for themselves.

Preventive-based leaders emphasize collaborative problem-solving, with leaders and employees working to identify and solve problems. A preventive-based leader may implement a Kaizen program to encourage employees to identify and address issues continuously (Ishikawa, 2013). In contrast, an autocratic leader may focus more on making decisions without involving employees.

What Are The Importance And Benefits Of Prevention-Based Leadership For High-Performance Teams...?

Let's discuss the benefits of prevention-based leadership for any organization, such as the ability to improve morale. When leaders take a proactive approach to problem-solving and actively work to prevent problems, employees feel more secure and confident in their roles. This can eventually lead to higher levels of job satisfaction, lower turnover rates, and increased loyalty to the organization (Cheng et al., 2020). it creates a more secure and confident work environment for employees. Thus, employees will feel that their leaders are actively invested in their well-being, taking steps to identify and address potential problems before they become significant.

This sense of security can lead to higher levels of job satisfaction, as employees feel they are working in an environment where their leaders are supportive and proactive. This can also lead to lower turnover rates, as employees are more likely to stay with an organization where they feel valued and supported (Cheng et al., 2020).

Furthermore, when leaders take a preventive approach, it can increase employees' loyalty to the organization. This is because employees feel that their leaders are invested in the organization's long-term success and are taking steps to ensure its continued growth and prosperity. This sense of loyalty can lead to increased commitment and dedication among employees, which can translate into higher levels of productivity and innovation (Kim & Lee, 2020).

Prevention-based leadership can also increase employee engagement by involving employees in problem-solving and decision-making. By giving employees a voice and empowering them to make decisions, leaders can increase their engagement and commitment to the organization. This can lead to higher productivity, creativity, and innovation (Kim & Lee, 2020).

Employees feel valued and recognized for their expertise and contributions in decision-making processes. This, in turn, will increase their sense of ownership and commitment to the organization's goals and objectives. Prevention-based leaders often create a culture of trust and transparency, which can help foster employee engagement.

A preventive-based leader may hold regular team meetings to discuss potential problems and solutions. They may encourage employees to share their perspectives and ideas and actively listen to their feedback. As such, leaders can tap into their diverse knowledge and expertise by involving employees in decision-making, leading to better problem-solving and decision-making outcomes.

In addition, prevention-based leaders often provide opportunities for professional development and growth, which can also increase employee engagement. They may offer training and mentorship programs, encourage employees to take on new challenges and responsibilities and provide feedback and recognition for their achievements.

Studies have shown engaged employees are more productive, creative, and innovative. They are also likelier to stay with their organization, leading to lower turnover rates and reduced recruitment costs (Gallup, 2017). By implementing a prevention-based leadership approach, high-performance leaders can create a culture of engagement and commitment, leading to better outcomes for the organization and its employees.

Conversations

The following are three straightforward conversations that portray the effectiveness of prevention-based leadership.

Conversation 1: Customer and Customer Service Representative

> **Customer:** Hi, I have been having issues with your product lately.
>
> **CSR**: I am sorry to hear that. Can you please provide me with more information about the issue?
>
> **Customer:** Sure, the product seems to break down after several uses.
>
> **CSR:** I see. We have been receiving similar complaints. We are working on a solution and will update you soon. In the meantime, we can provide you with a replacement product that has been tested and works perfectly.
>
> **Customer:** Thank you for your quick response. I appreciate it.
>
> **CSR:** No problem. We value your feedback and want to ensure your satisfaction with our products.

Conversation 2: Manager and Employee

> **Manager**: Hi, I noticed you need help to meet your targets.
>
> **Employee**: Yes, I have been struggling with some of the new procedures.
>
> **Manager**: I understand. Can you please provide me with more details about the specific areas you are struggling with?
>
> **Employee**: Sure. I need help understanding the new software system.

Manager: I see. I can arrange a training session to help you get up to speed with the new system. We want to ensure you have all the necessary resources to succeed in your role.

Employee: Thank you. I appreciate your support.

Manager: No problem. We value your contributions to the team and want to help you succeed.

Conversation 3: Two Employees

Employee 1: Hi, have you heard about the new project we are working on?

Employee 2: Yes, I have. It sounds exciting.

Employee 1: Definitely. I am worried about meeting the deadlines, though.

Employee 2: I understand. Is there anything I can do to help?

Employee 1: Actually, that would be great. Can you review some of my work and provide some feedback?

Employee 2: Sure, I would be happy to help. We are all in this together and want to ensure the project's success.

Employee 1: Thank you, I appreciate it.

Employee 2: No problem. We must support each other and work as a team to achieve our goals.

CHAPTER 2

A TOOL FOR PREVENTION-BASED LEADERSHIP

"Reflective listening is the key that unlocks the door to understanding, connection, and transformative leadership." –

Brené Brown

Reflective listening, a tool used by preventive-based leaders, is a communication technique where the listener repeats or paraphrases the speaker's message to confirm understanding and demonstrate empathy. It helps to build trust between the speaker and the listener. It involves actively listening to the speaker and reflecting on their words to show that you have heard and understood them correctly. When you use reflective listening, you show the speaker that you are interested in what they say and try to understand their perspective. This can help to create a more positive and productive communication environment.

Reflective listening creates a safe and supportive environment for the speakers to express themselves. It helps build trust, mutual respect, and understanding between the listener and speaker. Reflective listening also helps clarify misunderstandings and reduces the likelihood of conflicts arising from miscommunication.

There are many different ways to use reflective listening in leadership. For example, you could use it to:

* *Understand your team members' concerns.* When having a one-on-one conversation with a team member, use reflective listening to show that you are listening to their concerns and understand their perspective. This can help to build trust and rapport, and it can also help you to resolve any issues that the team member is facing.

* *Gather feedback.* When conducting a team meeting or presentation, use reflective listening to gather feedback from your team members. This will help you understand how your team members feel about the project or the presentation and identify any areas for improvement.

* *Resolve conflict.* When conflict arises within your team, use reflective listening to help the team members understand each other's perspectives. This can help de-escalate the competition and find an acceptable resolution for everyone involved.

Here's An Example Of Reflective Listening In Action:

Suppose a team member comes to their supervisor and says, "I'm feeling overwhelmed with my workload and struggling to keep up with my deadlines." A reflective listener might respond by saying, "It sounds like you're feeling overwhelmed and struggling to keep up with your workload. Is that right?"

In this example, the listener has reflected on the speaker's message to them, confirming that they understand the situation correctly. This response can help the team member feel heard and understood, which can help reduce their stress and anxiety.

Here are some scenarios where reflective listening can be used in leadership:

During one-on-one meetings: Leaders can use reflective listening to build rapport and trust with their team members by actively listening to their concerns and reflecting on what they've heard. Suppose a manager is having a one-on-one conversation with an employee, feeling stressed about a project. In that case, the manager can use reflective listening to show that they are listening to the employee's concerns and understanding their perspective. The manager would then ask the employee how they can help to make the project less stressful.

In team meetings: Leaders can use reflective listening to ensure all team members feel heard and understood. They can paraphrase each team member's contribution to ensure everyone is on the same page. If a team leader presents a new project to the team, the team leader can use reflective listening to gather feedback from the team members. They may ask each team member what they think of the project and what they think are the challenges and opportunities.

In conflict resolution: The team leader uses reflective listening to help the team members understand each other's perspectives. The team leader then asks the team members how to resolve the conflict. Leaders can use reflective listening to de-escalate conflicts by actively listening to both sides and reflecting on each person's words. This can help reduce misunderstandings and find common ground.

During performance reviews: Leaders can use reflective listening to provide constructive feedback to their team members. They can paraphrase the team member's contributions, acknowledge their strengths, and provide guidance on areas for improvement. This approach can help team members feel heard and valued while improving their performance.

Leaders can use reflective listening in coaching and mentoring to help their team members grow and develop. They can listen actively, ask open-ended questions, and reflect on what they've heard to help team members identify their strengths and areas for improvement. This approach can build trust and help team members feel supported as they work towards their goals.

Reflective listening is helpful for more than achieving leadership goals in a professional setting. It can and should be used in personal relationships as well.

In Your Personal Life:

When talking to your spouse, partner, or children, use reflective listening to show that you are interested in what they say and try to understand their perspective. This can help to strengthen your relationships and create a more positive and supportive environment.

When talking to a friend or family member going through a difficult time, use reflective listening to show that you are there for them and care about what they are going through. This can help them to feel supported and understood.

When talking to someone who has a different opinion than you, use reflective listening to show that you are open to hearing their perspective. This can help build understanding and create a more respectful dialogue.

CHAPTER 3

STRATEGIES FOR IMPLEMENTING PREVENTION-BASED LEADERSHIP.

"Preventive-based leadership with reflective listening is the compass that guides us towards a future of informed decisions, empowered teams, and sustainable achievements." –

Amy Edmondson.

In today's fast-paced and unpredictable business environment, prevention-based leadership has become a popular approach to practical management. This proactive approach focuses on anticipating and preventing problems before they occur rather than just reacting to them. Leaders practicing prevention-based leadership are better equipped to address potential issues and create a proactive problem-solving culture.

However, prevention-based leadership requires a high degree of emotional intelligence. Leaders with high emotional intelligence can better manage their and team members' emotions, allowing them to anticipate and address potential issues proactively.

Developing Emotional Intelligence Skills

To become a prevention-based leader, it is essential to develop emotional intelligence skills. Here are some techniques that can help leaders improve their emotional intelligence:

Self-awareness: Self-awareness is the foundation of emotional intelligence. Leaders can increase their self-awareness by reflecting on their emotions, triggers, and behaviors. By identifying patterns and tendencies in their emotional responses, they can become more attuned to their feelings and better manage them. Here are some examples of how leaders can improve their self-awareness:

Reflect on emotions: Reflect on your positive and negative emotions. Journaling, meditation, or mindfulness practices can help you identify your emotional states and their underlying causes.

Seek feedback: Ask your colleagues or team members about your emotional reactions or behavior. This can help you gain insights into your blind spots or areas for improvement.

Practice self-reflection: Set aside regular time for self-reflection, where you can review your successes, challenges, and goals. This can help you identify behavioral or emotional patterns and adjust your approach accordingly.

Empathy: Empathy is the ability to understand and relate to other people's emotions and experiences. Leaders can develop empathy by actively listening to their team members, asking open-ended questions, and practicing perspective-taking. Leaders can build stronger relationships and prevent conflicts by putting themselves in the other person's shoes and seeing things from their perspective. Here are some examples of how leaders can develop empathy:

Active listening: Pay attention to what others say without interrupting or judging them. Show interest in their thoughts, feelings, and perspectives by asking open-ended questions and summarizing their points.

Perspective-taking: Put yourself in the other person's shoes and try to see things from their point of view. Consider their values, beliefs, and experiences and how they might influence their emotions or behaviors.

Emotional validation: Acknowledge and validate other people's emotions, even if you disagree. This can help them feel heard and understood and prevent misunderstandings or conflicts.

Social Skills: Social skills are communicating effectively, building relationships, and managing conflicts. Leaders can develop social skills by actively listening, giving and receiving feedback, and collaborating. Leaders can create a proactive problem-solving culture by communicating clearly and empathetically, building trust, and finding win-win solutions to problems. Here are some examples of how leaders can improve their social skills:

Effective communication: Use clear, concise, and empathetic language when communicating with others. Avoid using jargon or technical terms that others might not understand. Use active listening skills to ensure you fully understand what others are saying.

Conflict resolution: Develop strategies for managing conflicts, such as active listening, compromise, or collaboration. Encourage team members to communicate openly and respectfully and provide a safe environment where disputes can be addressed without fear of retribution.

Collaboration: Foster an environment where team members feel empowered to collaborate and work together on projects. Encourage cross-functional teams and provide opportunities for team-building activities.

The Win-Win Scenario

Creating a win-win scenario involves developing an approach that focuses on anticipating problems and addressing them proactively. Here are some examples of how leaders can create a win-win scenario:

Engage team members in problem-solving: Encourage team members to identify potential problems and develop solutions. This gives them ownership of the process and fosters a proactive problem-solving culture. For example, a leader could hold a brainstorming session where team members can share their ideas for improving a project or process.

Encourage open communication: Create an environment where team members feel comfortable sharing their concerns, ideas, and feedback. This helps prevent misunderstandings and conflicts and fosters a culture of transparency and collaboration. For example, a leader could hold regular one-on-one meetings with team members to discuss their progress, challenges, and goals.

Foster a culture of continuous improvement: Encourage team members to learn from their mistakes, share their successes, and strive for constant improvement. This helps create a culture of learning, growth, and innovation. For example, a leader could hold regular training sessions or workshops to help team members develop new.

Change Talk

Change talk is a type of language individuals use that reflects their readiness, willingness, and ability to change their behavior positively. Change talk can be identified by specific statements indicating a person's desire, ability, reasons, and need for change. For example, words such as "I want to change," "I'm willing to try something new," or "I know I need to do things differently" are all examples of change talk.

In reflective listening, change talk can be a powerful tool to help individuals explore and resolve their ambivalence toward changing their behavior. When using reflective listening, the listener's role is to help the speaker explore their thoughts and feelings about change and identify their reasons for wanting to change.

It's important to note that change talk should not be used to pressure or coerce someone into making a change they are not ready or willing to make. Reflective listening should always be done with empathy, respect, and a non-judgmental attitude.

Here are some tips on how to use change talk effectively in reflective listening:

Listen for change talk: Be attentive to the speaker's language and listen for statements indicating their readiness, willingness, and ability to change.

Reflect the change talk: Use reflective statements acknowledging and reinforcing the speaker's change talk. For example, "I hear that you're thinking about making a change," or "It sounds like you're ready to try something new."

Explore ambivalence: Encourage the speaker to explore their ambivalence towards making a change. Ask open-ended questions that help the speaker identify their reasons for wanting to change and any barriers preventing them.

Encourage self-efficacy: Acknowledge the speaker's strengths and past successes to help them build confidence and self-efficacy. Please encourage them to set achievable goals and develop a plan for action.

It's essential to use change talk in a way that is respectful and supportive of the speaker's autonomy and decision-making process. Reflective listening should never be used to coerce or manipulate someone into making a change they are not ready or willing to make.

Avoid arguing or debating: It's important to avoid discussing or debating with the speaker about their reasons for making a change. This can cause them to become defensive and resist change. Instead, try to understand their perspective and help them explore their reasons for wanting to change.

Avoid lecturing or giving advice: Reflective listening is not about telling the speaker what to do or giving them advice. Instead, it's about helping them explore their thoughts and feelings about change and develop their plan for making a change.

Use reflective listening to build rapport: Building rapport and a trusting relationship with the speaker is crucial for effective reflective listening. Use active listening skills to show you are fully present and engaged in the conversation. *Paraphrase the speaker's words*, use open-ended questions, and provide positive feedback to help them feel heard and understood.

Using change talk effectively in reflective listening can help individuals explore their ambivalence towards making a change, develop their confidence and self-efficacy, and create their plan for taking action. It's important to remember that change is a process and that individuals must feel motivated, confident, and supported to change their behavior. Reflective listening can be a powerful tool in helping individuals make positive changes.

Speaker: "I know I must quit smoking because it's affecting my health. I'm willing to try nicotine patches to help me quit."

Effective Listener: The listener could reflect on the speaker's change talk by saying, "It sounds like you're ready to take steps towards quitting smoking, and you're willing to try nicotine patches. What else do you think could help you quit smoking?"

Ineffective Listener: The listener could pressure the speaker by saying, "You need to quit smoking because it's bad for your health. Nicotine patches are the best way to quit. You should start using them now." This approach is likely to make the speaker defensive and resistant to change.

Example 2: Conversation about starting a new exercise routine

Speaker: "I want to start exercising regularly because I know it's good for my health. I'm going to start by going for a walk every morning."

Effective Listener: The listener could reflect on the speaker's change talk by saying, "It sounds like you're motivated to start exercising regularly, and you've already planned to go for a walk every morning. What else could help you stick to your new routine?"

Ineffective Listener: The listener could lecture the speaker by saying, "You need to start exercising regularly because it's good for your health. Walking is a great start, but you should also do strength training and cardio. You should aim for at least an hour of exercise every day." This approach is likely to overwhelm the speaker and make them feel discouraged.

Example 3: Conversation about reducing alcohol consumption

Speaker: "I know I drink too much, and it's causing problems in my relationships and work. But cutting back is hard because I always feel stressed and anxious. I'm worried I won't be able to cope without alcohol."

Effective use of change talk: The listener could reflect on the speaker's change talk by saying, "It sounds like you're aware of the negative impact alcohol is having on your life, but you're struggling to cut back because you use it as a coping mechanism for stress and anxiety. Can you think of other ways to cope with stress and anxiety that don't involve alcohol?"

Ineffective use of change talk: The listener could argue with the speaker by saying, "You need to stop drinking because it's causing problems in your life. You shouldn't use stress and anxiety as an excuse to drink. You need to learn to cope without alcohol." This approach is likely to make the speaker defensive and resistant to change.

Speaker: "I know I need to change because I'm not happy with my weight, and it's affecting my self-esteem. But I don't know where to start. I've tried diets before, but they never seem to work."

Effective use of change talk: The listener could reflect on the speaker's change talk by saying, "It sounds like you're ready to make a change and improve your self-esteem. Understandably, you feel overwhelmed by the idea of starting a diet. What other options do you think might work for you?"

Ineffective use of change:talk: The listener could advise the speaker by saying, "You need to start a low-carb diet because it's the most effective way to lose weight. It would help if you also started exercising every day. That's the only way you're going to see results." This approach is likely to make the speaker feel judged and discouraged.

<u>**Example 4**</u>: Conversation about improving work-life balance

Speaker: "I feel like I'm always working and never have time for myself or my family. But my job is so demanding, and I don't want to let my boss or colleagues down. I feel like I'm stuck."

Effective use of change talk: The listener could reflect on the speaker's change talk by saying, "It sounds like you value your job and your responsibilities, but you also want to prioritize your personal life. Can you think of ways to balance work and your personal life?"

Ineffective use of change talk: The listener could pressure the speaker by saying, "You need to set boundaries with work and prioritize your family and personal time. If you don't, you'll burn out and regret it later." This approach is likely to make the speaker feel guilty and overwhelmed.

Speaker: "I know I need to start saving for retirement, but it's hard to find the extra money. I feel like I'm barely making ends meet as it is."

Effective use of change talk: The listener could reflect on the speaker's change talk by saying, "It sounds like you recognize the importance of saving for retirement, but you're struggling to find the extra funds. What steps could you take to reduce your expenses or increase your income?"

Ineffective use of change talk: The listener could lecture the speaker by saying, "You need to start saving for retirement now because it's going to be too late later. It would be best to cut unnecessary expenses like eating out or shopping. You should also find a higher-paying job." This approach is likely to make the speaker feel criticized and frustrated.

In all the examples, effective use of change talk involves reflecting on the speaker's language, acknowledging their reasons for making a change, and encouraging them to explore their solutions. Ineffective use of change talk involves pressuring or lecturing the speaker and telling them what to do. By using reflective listening skills to support the speaker's autonomy and decision-making process, you can help them develop their plan for positive behavior changes.

Prevention-based leadership involving change talk, anticipates problems and taking proactive steps to prevent them from occurring in the first place. According to a study by Kim and Lim (2019), this focuses on creating a culture of prevention rather than reactive problem-solving and fosters a culture of communication and transparency. Leaders must understand that prevention is not just about avoiding adverse outcomes but also creating opportunities for growth, innovation, and success.

Influential prevention-based leaders prioritize long-term results and invest in research and development to identify potential risks, and they are open to new ideas and innovation (Baker, 2020). They also focus on continuous improvement by regularly evaluating their strategies (Joshi & Al-Ghamdi, 2020). Prevention-based leadership is not about avoiding risks but managing them proactively and effectively. Leaders can develop this culture by adopting the following strategies :

Focus on the long-term: Prevention-based leadership requires leaders to think beyond short-term goals and prioritize long-term outcomes. They need to be proactive and anticipate potential problems that may arise in the future.

For example, invest in research and development to identify potential risks and develop mitigation strategies. By doing so, the company can stay ahead of its competitors and avoid potential disruptions to its operations. Embrace leaders who are open to new ideas and innovation. Leadership must be willing to take calculated risks to achieve long-term goals.

Focus on continuous improvement: Prevention-based leadership requires leaders who are willing to learn from their mistakes and take corrective action to prevent them from happening again. For example, they regularly evaluate these strategies to refine their approach for better outcomes.

Taking ownership: Prevention-based leaders using change talk take ownership of their decisions and actions and are willing to take corrective action when necessary (Wu & Wu, 2020)

Foster a culture of trust: Prevention-based leadership requires leaders to foster a culture of trust and collaboration. They must be open and transparent in their communication and encourage employees to share their ideas and insights. For example, a leader who fosters a culture of trust may encourage employees to report potential problems and offer solutions to prevent them. Doing so can avoid potential issues and foster a sense of ownership and accountability among employees.

Effective communication is critical to preventing problems from occurring in the first place. Leaders can encourage communication and transparency by regularly sharing information, setting up open-door policies, and motivating team members to share their concerns and ideas. This helps create a culture of openness and collaboration, which can prevent misunderstandings and conflicts from arising.

Another way is to develop a risk management plan to identify and proactively address potential risks before they become problems. This technique would involve developing and enforcing that identify potential risks and support a preventive-based approach, such as evaluating their likelihood and impact and developing strategies to mitigate or prevent them. By taking a proactive approach to risk management, leaders can stop problems before they occur.

Leaders should also encourage continuous learning and development by investing in training and development programs for their team members. This learning method helps team members develop the skills and knowledge they need to identify potential problems and take proactive steps to prevent them. Leaders can create a team of proactive problem-solvers by fostering a continuous learning and development culture.

Leaders should also lead by example by modeling the behavior they want to see in their team members. This tactic includes taking a proactive approach to problem-solving, communicating effectively, and being transparent and open to feedback. By leading by example, leaders can inspire their team members to adopt a prevention-based leadership approach.

Yet, another way is to use data to make informed decisions about potential risks and opportunities. This method of making informed decisions involves collecting and analyzing data to identify trends and patterns that could indicate potential problems. By using data to make informed decisions, leaders can take proactive steps to prevent problems before they occur.

One way to use data is through Risk management: Many organizations use data to identify potential risks and develop strategies to manage them. For example, a financial institution may collect market trends and customer behavior data to identify potential hazards like loan defaults. By analyzing this data, the organization can develop strategies to mitigate those risks, such as adjusting lending criteria or increasing reserves to cover potential losses.

Another way to use data is to create a marketing strategy: Companies can also use data to inform their marketing strategies. By collecting data on customer demographics, behavior, and preferences, companies can identify trends and patterns that can help them develop more effective marketing campaigns. For example, a retailer may analyze sales data to determine which products are popular among certain age groups or geographic regions. They can then use this information to target specific customer segments with tailored marketing messages.

One other effective way is to use data to inform talent management decisions. Companies can identify top performers by analyzing employee performance data and developing retention strategies. They can also identify areas where employees may need additional training or support to improve performance. For example, a healthcare organization may analyze patient outcomes data to recognize nurses who consistently provide high-quality care. They can then give those nurses additional training or offer incentives to encourage them to stay with the organization.

Communication Skills

Leaders who can communicate effectively can prevent problems and conflicts from arising in the first place. We will discuss how leaders can use effective communication techniques such as active listening, conflict resolution, and collaboration to prevent problems and conflicts.

Active listening is an essential skill for effective communication. Leaders who actively listen to their colleagues and employees can prevent misunderstandings and conflicts. Tips for active listening include maintaining eye contact, asking clarifying questions, and summarizing what the speaker has said. (source: "Effective Communication Skills in the Workplace," National Association of State Personnel Executives)

Clarifying expectations is another essential communication technique for reflective leadership via prevention-based Leadership. Leaders should communicate expectations for job performance, roles, and responsibilities to prevent conflicts and misunderstandings. Leaders should communicate these expectations clearly and regularly and seek feedback to ensure they are understood. (source: "Effective Communication in the Workplace," Forbes)

Conflict resolution is a vital communication technique for leaders. When conflicts arise, leaders should be able to resolve them quickly and effectively. Leaders should listen to all parties involved, identify the conflict's root cause, and propose mutually acceptable solutions. (source: "Conflict Resolution Skills: Definition and Examples," Indeed)

Collaboration is another essential communication technique for reflective leadership via prevention-based Leadership. Leaders should encourage collaboration among team members and departments to prevent silos and conflicts. Leaders should facilitate communication among team members and encourage them to share ideas and feedback. (source: "Collaboration Skills: Definition and Examples," Indeed)

Here are some additional communication techniques that leaders can use to prevent problems and conflicts:

Empathy: Leaders should practice compassion by putting themselves in their colleagues' and employees' shoes. By understanding their perspectives, leaders can prevent misunderstandings and conflicts. (source: "The Importance of Empathy in Leadership," Harvard Business Review)

Feedback: Leaders should provide regular feedback to their colleagues and employees to prevent misunderstandings and conflicts. Feedback should be specific, constructive, and focused on behavior, not personality. (source: "Giving Effective Feedback: A Guide for Leaders," Harvard Business Review)

Transparency: Leaders should be transparent about their decisions, actions, and intentions. Transparency can prevent misunderstandings and conflicts by promoting trust and open communication. (source: "The Importance of Transparency in Leadership," Forbes)

Nonverbal communication: Leaders should be aware of their nonverbal communication, such as facial expressions and body language. Nonverbal cues can communicate messages that may contradict verbal communication, causing misunderstandings and conflicts. (source: "Understanding Nonverbal Communication in the Workplace," Verywell Mind)

Cultural sensitivity: Leaders should be aware of cultural differences and practice cultural sensitivity. Cultural differences can cause misunderstandings and conflicts, so leaders should educate their colleagues and employees about different cultures. (source:

"Cultural Sensitivity in the Workplace," Society for Human Resource Management)

Written communication: Leaders should practice effective written communication by using clear and concise language, avoiding jargon, and using appropriate tone and style. Effective written communication can prevent misunderstandings and conflicts by providing clarity and avoiding confusion. (source: "Effective Written Communication: A Guide for Leaders," Harvard Business Review)

Thinking

I have never heard anyone say, on any level of education, that they have attended a thinking course. Coursework in Mathematics, Logic, and History detail some strategies for thinking in their genres. Maybe I'm wrong, and someone can write to me and let me know, but I've never known a course to introduce the concept of thinking as a skill in the corporate, educational, or public sectors. The necessary leadership skills are planning, decision-making, problem-solving, creativity, and interpersonal relationships.

Thinking is critical in preventive-based leadership because it is essential in anticipating problems and identifying potential solutions. Leaders who think preventively must be proactive and anticipate potential issues before they occur. This preventive thinking requires high-level strategic thinking, creativity, and problem-solving skills. Preventive-based leaders must also be able to analyze data, evaluate risks, and make decisions based on available information. They also use the skill of reflective listening, actively listening to another person and reflecting on what they have said to ensure understanding.

Preventive-based leadership is often associated with proactive leadership, defined as "taking the initiative to anticipate, plan, and prevent problems before they occur" (Cameron & Green, 2012, p. 152). This approach requires high-level strategic thinking, problem-solving skills, and the ability to analyze data and evaluate risks. In a study conducted by Finkelstein and Hambrick (1990), they found that proactive leaders who anticipate problems and take action to prevent them are more successful than reactive leaders who wait for problems to arise before taking action.

If a leader is to act and speak reflectively, they must think continuously. Most people stop thinking and react, particularly in conversations. We respond in a split second and often regret what comes out of our mouths. (oops, I shouldn't have said that – how many times have you said that to yourself). Very few decisions must be made in a split second without taking time to think. However, we never seem to connect thinking with listening.

When entering a conversation, people do not take the time to take in the view. They begin judging what they hear as if they already know all there is to know. Leaders need to take the time to explore various aspects of any conversation. One way to explore this is to use "zero-based thinking," which requires one to begin a conversation without preconceived notions. Most will read this as not even plausible, never mind possible. So here are some techniques that can be employed at the beginning of any conversation. Consider all of the relevant factors or ingredients to the conversation or situation. Think of all the inherent risks involved, and don't leave anything considered unimportant. That would be "pre-judging." List any alternatives that come to mind. This will cause those that are most obvious or likely to be used.

Use these in your conversations with the speaker. It doesn't place a burden on the speaker, nor does it promise how their input will be used. The thinking makes the responses you have focused.

Reflective listening also involves thinking but in a different way. According to the International Association of Facilitators (2018), reflective listening involves "focusing on the speaker, clarifying their thoughts and feelings, and reflecting what you hear to ensure mutual understanding." This approach requires thinking differently from preventive-based leadership, focused on empathy, understanding, and active listening. Reflective listening requires the leader to be fully present in the moment, actively listen to the speaker, and reflect on what they have heard to ensure understanding... Reflective listening also involves considering the speaker's perspective, feelings, and needs.

There is a preconceived notion that the human mind is naturally creative. Let's debunk that right here. The human mind is uncreative and works best when established patterns link new information to what is already known. Although applying yesterday's thinking to today's situation is tempting, the new position may differ significantly from the old. That is why conditions and assumptions must be challenged. One must think of how a situation would be if the premise were absent or untrue. Then, take that into your open-ended conversations. It will make a difference. Don't, however, confuse challenge for change-talk.

Here is a way to constantly challenge assumptions through thinking. It's called REVERSAL... Suppose someone you did not trust owed you $2500.00. He gave you a check for the amount he owed and left town. When you go to the bank, you discover he only has a balance of $2450.00. We all know the bank will not cash your check. Yet, if you focus on how to get the money out of the bank, you may miss the creative solution. Now, reverse your thinking and your focus. If you deposit $51.00 in the account (you have the account and routing number and can fill out a deposit slip), the new balance will reflect 2501.00, and the check will clear.

Here Is something I've heard for a long time, particularly in a court of law or anywhere there is a discussion to be had – Complex problems require complex solutions arrived at via complex thinking." The reverse is more likely to be true. In any conversation, human beings must be able to unite, consolidate, and refine their thinking to extract the true importance of the issue. If leaders simplify their thinking, better questions can be asked and answered.

Listening

Just as thinking is a skill that must be practiced, listening is also a skill that must be practiced effectively in everyday conversations. This can improve communication and relationships with others. Several techniques and strategies can help individuals improve their listening skills. An effective way to learn how to listen in everyday conversations is by seeking opportunities to practice active listening skills. This can involve engaging in conversations with friends, family, and colleagues while consciously employing active listening techniques, such as paying attention, showing interest, providing feedback, and being non-judgmental. One helpful resource that offers practical guidance on listening effectively in everyday conversations is the book "Active Listening: Improve Your Ability to Listen and Lead" by Michael H. Hoppe (2015).

The book "Active Listening "provides a comprehensive guide to becoming a better listener in personal and professional settings. Hoppe emphasizes the importance of active listening, which involves entirely focusing on the speaker, understanding their perspective, and responding appropriately. The book provides practical tips and strategies for active listening, including:

1) Pay attention: Attention to the speaker and eliminating distractions are essential for an effective listener. The book guides how to focus on the speaker, maintain eye contact, and avoid interrupting.

2) Show interest: Demonstrating interest in the speaker and their message can improve communication and build relationships. Hoppe explains how to show interest through body language, asking questions, and summarizing the speaker's message.

3) Provide feedback: Feedback to the speaker can help clarify their message and ensure mutual understanding. The book guides how to provide feedback through paraphrasing, reflecting on feelings, and asking for clarification.

4) Be non-judgmental: Avoiding judgment and showing empathy can create a safe and open communication environment. Hoppe explains how to be non-judgmental through active listening, asking open-ended questions, and refraining from offering advice.

Additionally, seeking feedback from others can be a valuable tool for improving listening skills. Asking others for feedback on how well you listened during a conversation can help identify areas for improvement and provide motivation to continue practicing active listening techniques.

Another valuable resource for learning to listen effectively is the TED talk"5 Ways to Liste ton Bette" by Julian Treasure. In the talk, Treasure outlines five critical techniques for effective listening:

Silence: Taking a moment of silence before listening can help clear the mind and focus on the speaker.

The mixer: Paying attention to the different sounds and voices in a conversation can help improve listening skills.

Savoring: Enjoying the sound of someone's voice and focusing on the meaning of their words can help improve listening skills.

Listening positions: Choosing the correct listening position can help improve communication and understanding.

RASA: This acronym stands for Receive, Appreciate, Summarize, and Ask, which are critical steps in effective listening

Furthermore, seeking professional development opportunities such as workshops, seminars, or courses can help individuals learn and refine their listening skills. These opportunities can provide a more structured, focused approach to learning and practicing active listening techniques.

I am giving Feedback – reflectively.

How do you give feedback reflectively? It is an essential but challenging task. Having a discussion, particularly an argument, is one of the most selfish activities in which a human being can participate. Think of it: during an argument or a heated debate, are you making a point for the speaker or yourself? Are you even thinking about how they will feel once the abuse has left your brain and messaged through your lips? We often do not think of what we will say; we say it and deal with the consequences afterward.

Leaders who give reflective feedback use an approach centered on helping the recipient understand the impact of their behavior and actions on others. It is focused on creating a safe and open environment where individuals can reflect on their performance, identify areas for improvement, and take action to make positive changes. In this section, we will explore five examples of how to give feedback reflectively.

Begin with a positive comment: it sets the tone for the conversation and establishes trust between the giver and the receiver. It helps to create a safe and supportive environment where the recipient is more likely to be open and receptive to the feedback. Before providing feedback, it is essential to establish a positive tone. Start by highlighting something positive about the recipient's behavior or performance. For example, "I appreciate your commitment to meeting deadlines, and I noticed that you submitted the report on time." This positive comment helps reinforce the beneficial behaviors that the recipient has exhibited and encourages them to continue to demonstrate those behaviors. It is an opportunity to acknowledge the recipients' strengths and contributions to the team, which can help to build their confidence and motivation.

Another example is if you give feedback to an employee struggling with a particular task, you could begin the conversation by saying, "*I appreciate your effort and dedication to this project. I noticed you have been working hard to meet the deadline, and I appreciate your commitment.*" This statement acknowledges the employees' work and shows that their effort has not gone unnoticed.

The positive comment must be genuine and specific. It should not be used to manipulate or soften the feedback that follows. It is also vital to ensure that the positive comment is clear and concise, as it may appear insincere or meaningless.

Describe the behavior: Describing the behavior in detail is essential to giving reflective feedback. It helps ensure the recipient understands precisely what they did or said that was problematic. It also helps to keep the feedback objective and free from personal biases or assumptions.

When describing the behavior, it is crucial to be specific and provide details about what was observed. This can include information about the timing, location, and context of the behavior, as well as any other relevant information that can help to clarify the situation.

For example, if you give feedback to an employee who interrupted a colleague during a meeting, you could describe the behavior in the following way: "*During the meeting yesterday, I observed that when Judy was speaking, you interrupted her and raised your voice. This happened twice during the meeting, and it seemed to make Judy uncomfortable. She stopped speaking and didn't continue until you had finished.*"

This description details the behavior and its impact on the recipient. It avoids making assumptions or judgments about the individual's intentions or motivations and instead focuses on the observable facts.

It is important to note that when describing the behavior, it is crucial to remain objective and avoid using emotional or judgmental language. This can help to ensure that the feedback is perceived as constructive and not as an attack on the recipient.

Describing the impact of the behavior or action is critical in providing feedback reflectively. This helps the recipient understand the consequences of their behavior and how it affects others. It is essential to describe the impact objectively and focus on the observable effects.

When describing the impact, using specific examples and avoiding making generalizations or assumptions is essential. It is also important to be sensitive to the feelings of others and to avoid language that could be perceived as judgmental or critical.

For example, if an employee interrupted a colleague during a meeting, you could describe the impact as follows: *"When you interrupted Jane, it made her feel disrespected and silenced. This interruption also disrupted the meeting flow and made it difficult for others to contribute. Several team members appeared uncomfortable and hesitant to speak up after your interruption."*

By describing the impact in this way, you are providing specific details about the consequences of the behavior. You are also helping the recipient to understand how their actions affected others in the meeting. This can help the recipient to see the importance of their behavior and the need to change it.

Conversations

Conversation 1:

> **Customer**: I want to speak to a manager. Your product is terrible, and it's caused me a lot of problems.

Sales Rep: I'm sorry you've had a bad experience with our product. Can you tell me more about what went wrong?

Customer: What's the point? You, people, will give me the runaround like you always do.

Sales Rep: I understand that you're frustrated, and I apologize for any inconvenience we've caused. I assure you I'm here to help you and find a solution. Can you give me more details about the issue you're experiencing?

Customer: Fine. The product doesn't work as advertised, and it's caused me a lot of financial loss.

Sales Rep: I see. We want our customers to have a better experience than that. Let's see if we can find a solution that works for you. Can I ask some questions about your system to understand the issue better?

Customer: Okay, go ahead.

Sales Rep: Thank you. First, tell me more about your system's specifications and requirements. That will help us better understand what's causing the compatibility issue.

Customer: I've already told you that the product doesn't work! Why can't you fix it?

Sales Rep: I understand that you're frustrated, but to find a solution, we need to understand the root of the problem. Can you please provide more information about your system so we can find the best solution?

Customer: Fine. It's a Windows 10 system with 8 GB of RAM and a 500 GB hard drive.

Sales Rep: Thank you for that information. Let's see if our product needs any specific system requirements. In the meantime, can you provide me with the product serial number so I can look up more information about it?

In this conversation, the sales rep uses preventive-based leadership by taking ownership of the customer's issue and actively seeking a solution. They also use reflective listening by acknowledging the customer's frustration and asking clarifying questions to better understand the problem.

Conversation 2:

Customer: I need to speak to a manager. Your company has the worst customer service I've ever experienced.

Sales Rep: I'm sorry to hear that you're not satisfied with our customer service. Can you tell me more about what specifically went wrong?

Customer: I've been on hold for over an hour, and no one has been able to help me with my issue.

Sales Rep: I understand that being on hold for a long time can be frustrating. Before escalating to a manager, let me see if I can assist you with your issue. What is the problem you're experiencing?

Customer: I need to cancel my service, but I can't seem to do it online or over the phone.

Sales Rep: I see. Let me look into your account and see what options are available. While I'm doing that, can you tell me more about why you're looking to cancel?

Customer: I'm unhappy with the service and found a better deal with a competitor.

Sales Rep: I see. Can you tell me more about what you're looking for in a service provider? We can find a solution that works for you.

Customer: I'm just looking for better value and customer service. Your company doesn't seem to care about its customers.

Sales Rep: I apologize if you feel that way. We value our customers and want to provide the best service possible. Let's see if we can offer promotions or discounts to meet your needs better. In the meantime, let me know what I can do to help you cancel your service.

In this conversation, the sales rep uses preventive-based leadership by taking ownership of the customer's issue and attempting to find a solution before escalating to a manager. They also use reflective listening by acknowledging the customer's frustration and asking clarifying questions to better understand the issue without telling the customer the word "No."

Conversation 3 :

Sales Rep: I'm sorry you're experiencing issues with our product. Can you tell me more about what precisely isn't working for you?

Customer: It seems like it's not as efficient as it should be. I spend more time trying to make it work than getting things done.

Sales Rep: I understand. It sounds like you're looking for a product to help you be more productive and efficient. Have you considered trying our XYZ product instead? It's designed to streamline tasks and improve productivity for users.

Customer: I haven't heard of that one. Is it better than this one?

Sales Rep: Well, it's different, and it might be a better fit for your needs. It's received great feedback from other customers looking for a similar solution. Would you be interested in learning more about it?

By using reflective listening, the sales rep could understand the customer's concerns and offer a potential solution without admitting fault or telling the customer no. By highlighting the benefits of the XYZ product and addressing the customer's specific pain points, the sales rep may be able to make a new sale.

Conversation 4:

Sales Rep: I'm sorry you had a negative experience with our customer service team. Can you tell me more about what happened?

Customer: They were so unhelpful, and I don't want to do business with a company that treats its customers that way.

Sales Rep: I completely understand your frustration. Our customer service team is usually accommodating and friendly. If you don't mind me asking, what were you trying to accomplish when you reached out to them?

Customer: I was having trouble with my account and needed some assistance.

Sales Rep: I see. It sounds like you were trying to resolve an issue with your account. If you're open to it, I'd be happy to assist with any questions or concerns you have about your account. Is there anything specific you'd like me to look into?

Customer: I want to ensure everything is okay with my account.

Sales Rep: Of course, I'm happy to help with that. Let me look and see if there are any issues or concerns I can address for you. While doing that, can I tell you about any other products or services we offer that might interest you?

By using reflective listening, the sales rep could understand the customer's concerns and offer assistance without admitting fault or telling the customer no. By focusing on the customer's needs and addressing their specific concerns, the sales rep may be able to make a new sale.

CHAPTER 4

THE ROLE OF EMOTIONAL INTELLIGENCE IN PREVENTION-BASED LEADERSHIP.

"Emotional intelligence is the ability to sense, understand, and effectively apply the power and acumen of emotions as a source of human energy, information, connection, and influence." –

Robert K. Cooper.

As we've discussed, leadership is a crucial aspect of any organization, and leaders are responsible for creating a vision, setting objectives, and guiding their teams toward achieving those goals. Prevention-based leadership is a style of leadership that focuses on preventing problems from arising rather than reacting to them after they occur. Emotional intelligence, believe it or not, plays a critical role in prevention-based leadership, enabling leaders to connect with their teams on a deeper level, anticipate potential issues, and make informed decisions.

The Role Of Emotional Intelligence In Prevention-Based Leadership

I was a young football coach in 1986, coaching a pee-wee team in the Buddy Young Football League, based in Harlem, NY. The only thing I knew about coaching then was the firebrand I was introduced to by my high school and college coaches and the formation and Wishbone playbooks I had from my experiences. A coach was to be tough, yelling at officials, players, and even parents when warranted. I took some of those lessons from the gridiron and used them in business: never to back down, always show strength, and be determined, among others. How did it work for me? Well, let's see, our team was undefeated with only 7 points scored in two seasons, and professionally, I was among the fastest to move up to management with my employer. I wish I had a mentor to tell me to slow down. Your leadership is not determined by the fire in your belly but by the empathy in your actions and heart. It took me quite some time and many mistakes to develop emotional intelligence and use it in my future leadership roles.

Emotional intelligence is the ability to recognize and understand emotions in oneself and others and use this knowledge to guide thought and behavior effectively. As a prevention-based leader, one must be proactive and anticipate potential issues before they arise. Emotional intelligence plays a different but critical role in this leadership style, as it enables leaders to connect with their team members on a deeper level, understand their emotions, and anticipate potential problems.

Leaders with high emotional intelligence are better equipped to handle stressful situations, resolve conflicts, and communicate effectively with their team members. Emotional intelligence allows leaders to respond appropriately to their team members' emotions, improving team morale, motivation, and productivity. Emotionally intelligent leaders are likelier to inspire their team members and build a positive work culture. It would have been an excellent tool for me as a call center manager when I had to calm an entire staff due to a bomb threat shortly after the World Trade Center attack in early 2000. The threat turned out to be nothing, just a prank call, but we lost an entire night of business because the manager did not handle the matter with empathy and emotional intelligence.

Reflective Listening And Emotional Intelligence

As we know, reflective listening involves actively listening to another person and reflecting on what they have said to ensure that both parties have a shared understanding. Reflective listening is an essential skill for leaders, enabling them to connect with their team members on a deeper level and understand their emotions.

Leaders who practice reflective listening are more likely to build emotional trust and bond with their team members, which improves communication, collaboration, and productivity. These combined techniques also allow leaders to demonstrate empathy, a crucial aspect of emotional intelligence. By understanding and acknowledging their team members' emotions, leaders can build stronger relationships with their team members and create a more positive work environment.

Emotional intelligence is crucial to any high-performance leader. It enables one to connect with team members, anticipate potential problems, and make informed decisions. Leaders with high emotional intelligence are better equipped to handle stress, manage their emotions effectively, and inspire their team members to achieve their best.

Emotional intelligence also enables high-performance leaders to build strong relationships with their team members. When leaders are emotionally intelligent, they can better understand their team members' emotions and respond appropriately. This can improve team morale, motivation, and productivity, as team members feel valued and supported by their leader.

The Connection Between Emotional Intelligence And Resilience

Prevention-based leaders must also be resilient, bounce back from setbacks, and adapt to change effectively. Emotional intelligence is critical in resilience, enabling leaders to manage their emotions effectively and respond to stressful situations appropriately. Leaders with high emotional intelligence are better equipped to handle setbacks and adapt to change, which can improve their performance and team performance. Only some coaches on a ballfield or part of a business team can bring home a winner. There are setbacks, sometimes overwhelming, every day. Those leaders with preventive and emotional intelligence will rise and lead their teams to success.

Emotional intelligence also enables leaders to build resilience in their team members. By understanding their team members' emotions and responding appropriately, leaders can support their team members through difficult times, enabling them to bounce back from setbacks and adapt to change effectively.

In conclusion, emotional intelligence plays a critical role in prevention-based leadership. Leaders with high emotional intelligence are better equipped to connect with their team members, anticipate potential problems, and make informed decisions. Reflective listening is an essential skill for leaders, as it enables them to understand their team members' emotions and respond appropriately, building trust and empathy. Emotional intelligence is also crucial for high-performance leaders, allowing them to achieve exceptional results consistently and build strong relationships with their team members.

Furthermore, emotional intelligence is connected to resilience, enabling leaders to manage their emotions effectively and appropriately respond to setbacks and change. By building strength in their team members, leaders can support their team members through difficult times and enable them to bounce back and adapt effectively.

Prevention-based leadership is becoming increasingly important in today's complex and fast-paced work environment. Emotionally intelligent leaders are better equipped to handle this leadership style's challenges and create a positive work environment that enables their team members to achieve their full potential.

CHAPTER 5

MEASURING SUCCESS VS POTENTIAL CHALLENGES - HOW HIGH-PERFORMANCE LEADERS CAN MEASURE THE SUCCESS OF THEIR PREVENTION-BASED LEADERSHIP

"Measuring progress is important to determine the success of any leadership approach. Without measurement, it is impossible to know if you are achieving your goals and making progress." –

John C. Maxwell.

Prevention-based leadership focuses on preventing problems before they arise. High-performance leaders who use this approach are proactive and strategic, focusing on risk management, anticipating potential issues, and creating a positive and productive work environment for their team members.

Measuring the success of prevention-based leadership can be challenging. Unlike traditional leadership approaches, prevention-based leadership is about avoiding problems rather than reacting to them. As a result, there may be more effective ways to measure success than standard metrics, such as financial performance and productivity.

To measure the success of prevention-based leadership, high-performance leaders can use reflective listening and other methods to gather feedback from their team members, track key performance indicators (KPI's), and identify potential challenges and opportunities for improvement.

Reflective Listening For Measuring Success

Reflective listening is a technique that involves actively listening to feedback from others, considering their perspective, and responding in a way that demonstrates empathy and understanding. High-performance leaders can use reflective listening to gather feedback from their team members and measure the success of their prevention-based leadership.

By engaging in reflective listening, leaders can gain insight into how their team members feel about their work, how they perceive their leader's actions, and what improvements they would like to see. This information can be used to adjust leadership strategies and improve the overall effectiveness of prevention-based leadership.

To effectively use reflective listening, high-performance leaders should create a safe space for team members to provide feedback. This can involve regularly scheduled one-on-one meetings, open-door policies, and anonymous feedback mechanisms. By creating an environment where team members feel comfortable sharing their thoughts and ideas, high-performance leaders can gain valuable insight into the effectiveness of their prevention-based leadership.

Key Performance Indicators (Kpi's) And Other Metrics

High-performance leaders can also use key performance indicators (KPI's) and other metrics to measure the success of their prevention-based leadership. While traditional metrics may not be the most effective way to measure prevention-based leadership, there are still metrics that can provide valuable insight into this leadership style's effectiveness.

For example, KPI's can include metrics related to employee engagement, such as employee satisfaction and retention rates. High-performance leaders can also track metrics related to risk management, such as the number of incidents that were prevented or the success rate of risk mitigation strategies. By monitoring these KPI's and other metrics, high-performance leaders can gain valuable insight into the effectiveness of their prevention-based leadership and make adjustments as needed.

Overcoming Challenges And Providing Solutions

While prevention-based leadership has many benefits, it has its challenges. High-performance leaders may need support from team members who are used to traditional leadership approaches or encounter roadblocks in implementing prevention-based strategies.

To overcome these challenges, high-performance leaders must be proactive and strategic. They should communicate the benefits of prevention-based leadership to their team members and provide training and support to help them adjust to this leadership style.

Leaders can also work to address specific challenges and provide solutions. For example, if team members resist prevention-based strategies, leaders can provide more education and training to help team members understand the benefits of this approach. If there are roadblocks in implementing a prevention-based strategy, leaders can work with their team members to identify and address these challenges.

Measuring the success of prevention-based leadership can be challenging. Still, high-performance leaders can use reflective listening, KPI's, and other metrics to gain valuable insight into the effectiveness of their leadership approach. By creating a safe space for team members to provide feedback, tracking relevant KPI's, and proactively addressing challenges, high-performance leaders can successfully implement prevention-based leadership and create a positive and productive work environment for their team members.

CHAPTER 6

"THE FUTURE IS NOT ABOUT TECHNOLOGY; IT'S ABOUT PEOPLE.

Prevention-based leadership is not about telling people what to do; it's about inspiring and empowering them to prevent problems before they arise." –

Simon Sinek

Prevention-based leadership emphasizes proactive risk management and creating a positive and productive work environment. Prevention-based administration is also evolving to meet these changes and challenges as the workplace becomes with new technologies, cultural shifts, and other factors.

Let's now explore the future of prevention-based leadership, how it is creating new technologies and cultural shifts, and what leaders can do to adapt and thrive in this changing landscape.

New Technologies And Prevention-Based Leadership

One method describing how the future of prevention-based leadership is likely to be shaped is through digital feedback tools. As organizations increasingly become digitized, the importance of real-time feedback and data analytics cannot be overstated. Digital feedback tools can enable leaders to gather feedback from team members in real time and thus quickly identify potential issues and areas for improvement. By leveraging this technology, leaders can take a proactive approach to risk management, allowing them to address issues before they escalate into major problems.

Digital feedback tools can also provide leaders with analytics and other metrics that can help measure the effectiveness of their prevention-based leadership approach. Using data analytics, leaders can track performance metrics and key performance indicators (KPI's) that can provide insights into team dynamics, employee engagement, and overall organizational health. By analyzing these metrics, leaders can identify areas for improvement and adjust their prevention-based leadership approach accordingly.

Another technology that is likely to enhance prevention-based leadership is artificial intelligence (AI). AI can analyze large amounts of data, enabling leaders to identify patterns and trends that may not be apparent through manual analysis. AI can also help leaders predict potential issues and proactively prevent them. For example, AI-powered tools can analyze employee satisfaction levels and identify employees at risk of leaving the organization. This information can be used by leaders to proactively address the concerns of those employees and prevent them from exiting the organization.

However, it is essential to note that technology is not a substitute for human interaction and communication. While digital feedback tools and AI can be valuable tools for prevention-based leadership, leaders must continue cultivating solid relationships with their teams and practice reflective listening. Leaders must remember that digital tools cannot replace face-to-face interactions and human empathy. As such, technology should be seen as a complement to, rather than a replacement for, interpersonal communication.

These technologies can enable leaders to gather real-time feedback, track performance metrics, and predict potential issues, thereby helping them take a proactive risk management approach. However, it is essential to remember that technology is not a substitute for human interaction and communication. High-performance leaders must continue cultivating solid relationships with their teams and practice reflective listening to ensure their prevention-based leadership approach remains effective.

Cultural Shifts And Prevention-Based Leadership

Cultural shifts are a significant factor impacting the evolution of prevention-based leadership. As societal values and norms change, high-performance leaders must adapt their leadership styles to meet the changing needs of their team members. One such cultural shift is the increasing focus on employee well-being and mental health. In recent years, there has been a growing awareness of how workplace stress and burnout can impact employee well-being and mental health. We have all witnessed, if not been a part of, workplace stress and how it affects performance from calls to meetings, both in person and virtually. Prevention-based leaders must be mindful of this cultural shift and the impact of their leadership style on their team members' mental health and well-being.

Prevention-based leaders can focus on creating a positive and supportive work environment to adapt to this cultural shift. This can involve implementing policies and practices prioritizing a work-life balance, offering team members mental health support and resources, and promoting a culture of open communication and empathy. For example, leaders can encourage team members to take breaks throughout the day, offer flexible work arrangements, and provide resources such as Employee Assistance Programs (EAPs) to support mental health. Leaders can also promote open communication and empathy by actively listening to their team members and creating a safe space for them to express their concerns.

Another cultural shift impacting prevention-based leadership is the increasing emphasis on diversity, equity, and inclusion. In recent years, there has been a growing awareness of the importance of creating a work environment where all team members feel valued and included. High-performance leaders must proactively address issues related to diversity and inclusion and create a work environment where all team members feel valued and included.

Prevention-based leaders can prioritize diversity and inclusion in their strategies to adapt to this cultural shift. This can involve implementing policies and practices that promote diversity and inclusion, offering training and education to team members on these topics, and actively seeking diverse perspectives and ideas. For example, leaders can implement diversity and inclusion training programs, create Employee Resource Groups (ERGs) to support underrepresented groups, and ensure that diverse perspectives are represented in decision-making processes. By prioritizing diversity and inclusion, leaders can create a work environment where all team members feel valued and included, improving overall team performance and morale.

Moreover, cultural shifts can be challenging, particularly for leaders with a more traditional leadership style. Leaders may face resistance from team members who resist change or who may need help understanding the importance of these cultural shifts. In such cases, leaders must communicate the importance of these cultural shifts and how they align with the organization's values and goals. Leaders can also engage with team members to better understand their concerns and perspectives, which can help to build trust and promote a culture of open communication.

Cultural shifts are a significant factor impacting the evolution of prevention-based leadership. High-performance leaders must adapt and proactively address these cultural shifts concerning employee well-being, mental health, diversity, equity, and inclusion. Leaders prioritizing prevention-based leadership must create a positive and supportive work environment that prioritizes work-life balance, mental health, open communication, and empathy. They must also actively promote diversity, equity, and inclusion in their leadership strategies to create a work environment where all team members feel valued and included. Ultimately, by navigating these cultural shifts successfully, leaders can create a work environment where team members feel supported, engaged, and empowered to achieve high performance levels.

Other Factors Impacting Prevention-Based Leadership

Other factors, such as economic trends, geopolitical shifts, and environmental concerns, also impact prevention-based leadership. High-performance leaders must be aware of these factors and adapt their leadership strategies accordingly.

For example, economic trends such as globalization and the increasing focus on sustainability are driving the need for leaders who can navigate complex global markets and address environmental concerns. High-performance leaders prioritizing prevention-based leadership must be mindful of these trends and adapt their leadership strategies to address these challenges.

Geopolitical shifts, such as the rise of populist movements and political instability in certain regions, also impact prevention-based leadership. High-performance leaders must be aware of these shifts and the potential risks they pose to their organization and be proactive in risk management and crisis planning.

Prevention-based leadership is a style of leadership that emphasizes proactive risk management and creating a positive and productive work environment. Prevention-based leadership is also evolving to meet these changes and challenges as the workplace grows with new technologies, cultural shifts, and other factors.

High-performance leaders prioritizing prevention-based leadership must be mindful of changes and adapt their leadership strategies to address these challenges. This may involve using new technologies to gather feedback and track performance metrics, promoting a culture of diversity and inclusion, and proactively addressing employee well-being and mental health issues.

By adapting to these changes and challenges, high-performance leaders can create a work environment that is productive, positive, and resilient. Prevention-based leadership can help organizations thrive in a rapidly changing world by empowering leaders to prevent problems before they arise and create a culture of continuous improvement.

The future of prevention-based leadership is bright as leaders continue to adapt and evolve to meet new challenges and opportunities. By staying ahead of the curve and being proactive in risk management, high-performance leaders can create a work environment that is productive, positive, and resilient. With this mindset, high-performance leaders can achieve great success in the future.

CHAPTER 7

CASE STUDIES, REAL-LIFE EXAMPLES, AND EXERCISES TO ENHANCE PREVENTION-BASED LEADERSHIP

It is helpful to examine case studies and real-life examples to understand better how prevention-based leadership using reflective listening can be successful in organizations. Additionally, incorporating exercises can provide an engaging and hands-on learning experience that can enhance the development of prevention-based leadership skills. This section will explore case studies, real-life examples, and exercises that can help leaders develop and implement prevention-based leadership strategies.

Case Studies

Case studies are a valuable tool for understanding how prevention-based leadership can be successful in organizations. By examining real-life examples, leaders can gain insights into the benefits of prevention-based leadership and the challenges that may arise.

Case Study 1: Johnson & Johnson

Johnson & Johnson is a pharmaceutical and healthcare company that has long been recognized for its commitment to prevention-based leadership. Yet, how it handled the Tylenol crisis is a case study in prevention-based leadership that has been studied extensively over the years. In 1982, seven people in Chicago died after taking Tylenol capsules laced with cyanide. The news of these deaths caused widespread panic and fear, as Tylenol was a popular and trusted pain reliever widely used by the public.

Johnson & Johnson, the parent company of Tylenol, responded to the crisis quickly and decisively. The company immediately recalled all Tylenol products from store shelves nationwide and worked with law enforcement and the FDA to investigate the source of the tampering. Johnson & Johnson also introduced tamper-resistant packaging for all of its Tylenol products, which became the industry standard for over-the-counter medications.

The company's response to the crisis was costly in the short term, resulting in the loss of millions of dollars in revenue and damage to the Tylenol brand. However, Johnson & Johnson demonstrated its commitment to prevention-based leadership by prioritizing the safety of its customers over its financial interests. By taking swift and decisive action to prevent harm, the company restored public trust and preserved the Tylenol brand's long-term success.

The Tylenol crisis is a powerful example of how prevention-based leadership can be successful in a crisis. Johnson & Johnson's response to the crisis prioritized proactive measures to prevent harm rather than simply reacting to the situation after the fact. By recalling all Tylenol products and introducing tamper-resistant packaging, the company could prevent further injury to its customers and demonstrate its commitment to their safety.

The Tylenol crisis also illustrates the importance of transparency and effective communication in prevention-based leadership. Johnson & Johnson's response to the problem was characterized by open and honest communication with the public, which helped to build trust and mitigate fears about the safety of Tylenol products. By being transparent about the situation and its response, Johnson

& Johnson was able to maintain the loyalty and trust of its customers, even in the face of a crisis.

Case Study 2: Google

Google is a technology company that has become well-known for its prevention-based leadership approach. In 2013, Google conducted a study to identify the qualities of high-performing teams. The study found that the most successful teams had a culture of psychological safety, where team members felt comfortable sharing their ideas and opinions without fear of retribution.

In response to this study, Google prioritized prevention-based leadership strategies that promoted psychological safety. This included implementing team-building exercises, offering training on effective communication and conflict resolution, and promoting a culture of empathy and respect. This case study illustrates how prevention-based leadership can improve team performance by prioritizing a supportive and inclusive work environment.

Real-life Examples

can also be helpful in understanding how prevention-based leadership can be successful in organizations. By examining real-world situations, leaders can gain insights into the practical applications of prevention-based leadership.

Real-life Example 1: Southwest Airlines

Southwest Airlines is an airline company that has become well-known for its prevention-based leadership approach. One example of this is the company's approach to customer service. Rather than waiting for customer complaints, Southwest Airlines encourages its employees to identify and address potential issues proactively.

This prevention-based approach has resulted in high levels of customer satisfaction and loyalty. By prioritizing proactive measures to prevent customer dissatisfaction, Southwest Airlines has built a strong brand reputation and stood out in a competitive market.

Real-life Example 2: Salesforce

Salesforce is a technology company that has prioritized prevention-based leadership in its approach to employee engagement. The company offers a range of benefits and resources to support employee well-being, including mental health support, flexible work arrangements, and opportunities for career growth.

By prioritizing prevention-based leadership strategies that prioritize employee wellbeing, Salesforce has been able to attract and retain top talent, leading to improved business performance.

Exercises

Incorporating exercises into leadership development programs can provide a hands-on learning experience that can enhance the development of prevention-based leadership skills. Leaders can use a few activities to develop their prevention-based leadership skills.

Exercise 1: Reflection and Goal Setting

One exercise that leaders can use to develop their prevention-based leadership skills is reflection and goal setting. This involves taking time to reflect on past experiences and identifying areas for improvement.

Example 3: Airbnb

Airbnb is an online platform that allows people to rent out their homes or apartments to travelers. The company has a prevention-based leadership approach that prioritizes transparency and open communication. The company believes that being transparent and honest with its employees can build trust and foster a culture of collaboration and innovation.

One example of this is the company's "transparency report." This report provides detailed information on how the company responds to government requests for user data and the number of incidents of discrimination reported on the platform. By being transparent about these issues, the company can build trust with its users and employees and demonstrate its commitment to creating a safe and inclusive venue.

In addition to transparency, Airbnb also prioritizes open communication. The company has several internal communication channels, including a company-wide email list and an online forum where employees can share ideas and feedback. The company also has a "listening tour" program, where executives visit different offices worldwide to listen to employee feedback and concerns.

As a result of these prevention-based leadership practices, Airbnb has built a culture of trust and collaboration. The company has been recognized for its commitment to diversity and inclusion, and its employees report high levels of job satisfaction and engagement.

Exercise:

1) Take a moment to reflect on your current leadership approach. Are there ways to be more transparent and open with your team members? How could you create more opportunities for open communication and feedback?

2) Think about a recent issue or challenge that arose in your organization. How did you respond to this issue? Could you have taken a more prevention-based approach? What steps could you take to prevent similar problems from arising?

3) Conduct a Team Health Assessment: One way to address issues within a team proactively is by regularly assessing the team's health. This can be done by gathering feedback from team members through anonymous surveys, focus groups, or one-on-one conversations. This exercise identifies areas where team members feel supported, and improvements

can be made. By identifying potential issues before they escalate, leaders can take preventative measures to address them.

4) Develop a Risk Management Plan: Leaders can work with their teams to identify potential risks and develop a plan to prevent them from occurring. This exercise involves brainstorming potential risks and developing strategies to mitigate them. For example, if the team relies heavily on one team member for a critical task, what happens if that team member is out of the office for an extended period? By identifying this risk, leaders can proactively develop a plan to cross-train team members to ensure continuity of work.

5) Create a Culture of Learning: Prevention-based leadership involves a commitment to continuous learning and improvement. Leaders can encourage a learning culture by providing opportunities for team members to learn new skills and develop their careers. This exercise involves identifying areas where team members would like to build their skills and creating opportunities for them. This could include providing training or mentorship opportunities, encouraging team members to attend conferences or networking events, or offering educational resources such as books or online courses.

REFERENCES

Baker, C. (2020). Prevention-Based Leadership:

What It Is and Why It Matters. Forbes. Retrieved from https://www.forbes.com/sites/forbescoachescouncil/2020/08/24/prevention-based-leadership-what-it-is-and-why-it-matters/

Basu, R., & Wright, J. N. (2018). Quality Beyond Six Sigma. Routledge.

Bennett, J., & Bennett, M. (2017). The Essential 5 Whys: A Proven Problem-Solving Technique for Business and Life. Lulu Press.

Burke, W. W., Rooks, G., & Coles, R. L. (2017). Project Management Leadership: Building Creative Teams. John Wiley & Sons.

Cheng, W., Liang, R., Li, X., & Li, C. (2020). The Effect of Preventive Leadership on Proactive Behavior: The Mediating Role of Job Crafting. Frontiers in Psychology, 11, 1-11.

Eriksson, P., & Kovalainen, A. (2015). Sustainability-Oriented Preventive Maintenance: An Empirical Study. Journal of Cleaner Production, 108, 60-68.

Gallup. (2017). State of the American workplace. Retrieved from https://www.gallup.com/workplace/238085/state-american-work-place-report-2017.aspx

Goh, S. K., & Elliott, C. (2018). The Impact of Prevention-Focused Leadership on Employee Creativity: The Moderating Role of Employee Regulatory Focus. Journal of Occupational and Organizational Psychology, 91(2), 410-432. doi: 10.1111/joop.12206

Hagen, S. (2018). Preventive Maintenance: Proactive Maintenance Strategies to Minimize Downtime. CRC Press.

Hartmann, T., Silbermann, M., Pröger, J., & Bader, Y. (2020). Preventive Leadership and Quality Management: Do They Interact to Enhance the Quality of Customer Service Delivery? International Journal of Quality & Reliability Management, 37(6), 1076-1093.

Ishikawa, K. (2013). What is Total Quality Control?: The Japanese Way. Prentice Hall.

Joshi, S. P., & Al-Ghamdi, A. S. (2020). Prevention-based Leadership: A Systematic Review. Journal of Business Research, 109, 212-221.

Kaplan, R. S. (2018). Risk Management and the Strategy Execution System. Harvard Business Review, 96(5), 80-89.

Kim, J., & Lim, J. (2019). Prevention-based Leadership and Employee Innovative Behavior: A Moderated Mediation Model. Journal of Business Research, 96, 224-235.

Kim, S., & Lee, S. (2020). The Effects of Preventive Leadership on Employee Engagement and Job Performance: The Mediating Role of Psychological Safety. International Journal of Environmental Research and Public Health, 17(20), 1-16.

Liu, Y., Huang, X., Zhang, Y., & Chen, Y. (2018). How Does Prevention-Focused Leadership Promote Employee Proactivity? The Mediating Role of Intrinsic Motivation and the Moderating Role of Power Distance Orientation. Journal of Business and Psychology, 33(5), 647-661. doi: 10.1007/s10869-017-9512-1

McGonagle, J. J., & Vella, K. (2018). Communicating to Manage risk. Routledge.

Montgomery, D. C. (2013). Introduction to Statistical Quality Control. John Wiley & Sons.

Rath, T., & Conchie, B. (2008). Strengths-based Leadership: Great leaders, teams, and why people follow. Gallup Press.

Schaufeli, W. B., Salanova, M., González-Romá, V., & Bakker, A. B. (2002). The Measurement of Engagement and Burnout: A Two Sample Confirmatory Factor Analytic Approach. Journal of Happiness Studies, 3(1), 71-92. doi: 10.1023/A:1015630930326

Stewart, G. L., & Clarke, S. (2018). Performance Management and Employee Well-Being. Routledge.

Wu, W. P., & Wu, Y. C. J. (2020). Prevention-based Leadership and Employee Outcomes: The Mediating Effects of Psychological Capital and the Moderating Effects of Regulatory Focus. Journal of Business Research, 117, 712-720

Chapter 3 References

"Collaboration Skills: Definition and Examples," Indeed. Retrieved from https://www.indeed.com/career-advice/career-development/collaboration-skills

"Conflict Resolution Skills: Definition and Examples," Indeed. Retrieved from https://www.indeed.com/career-advice/career-development/conflict-resolution-skills

"Cultural Sensitivity in the Workplace", Society for Human Resource Management. Retrieved from https://www.shrm.org/resourcesandtools/tools-and-samples/toolkits/pages/culturalcompetence.aspx

"Effective Communication in the Workplace," Forbes. Retrieved from https://www.forbes.com/sites/forbescoachescouncil/2019/06/18/effective-communication-in-the-workplace-14-proven-tips/?sh=53b0e06c-2e9a

"Effective Communication Skills in the Workplace," National Association of State Personnel Executives. Retrieved from https://www.naspe.net/effective-communication-skills-in-the-workplace.html

"Effective Written Communication: A Guide for Leaders," Harvard Business Review. Retrieved from https://hbr.org/2019/09/effective-written-communication-a-guide-to-style-and-tone

"Giving Effective Feedback: A Guide for Leaders," Harvard Business Review. Retrieved from https://hbr.org/2019/10/giving-effective-feedback-a-guide-for-leaders

"The Importance of Empathy in Leadership," Harvard Business Review. Retrieved from https://hbr.org/2020/05/the-importance-of-empathy-in-leadership

"The Importance of Transparency in Leadership," Forbes. Retrieved from https://www.forbes.com/sites/forbescoachescouncil/2018/04/09/the-importance-of-transparency-in-leadership/?sh=38d09f647c14

"Understanding Nonverbal Communication in the Workplace," Verywell Mind. Retrieved from https://www.verywellmind.com/understanding-nonverbal-communication-2795391

Cameron, K. S., & Green, M. (2012). Making Sense of Proactivity. In K. S. Cameron & G. M. Spreitzer (Eds.), The Oxford Handbook of Positive Organizational Scholarship (pp. 151-163). Oxford University Press.

Finkelstein, S., & Hambrick, D. C. (1990). Top-management-team Tenure and Organizational Outcomes: The Moderating Role of Managerial Discretion. Administrative Science Quarterly, 35(3), 484-503.

International Association of Facilitators. (2018). Reflective listening. Retrieved from https://www.iaf-world.org/site/resources/reflective-listening

Chapter 4 References

Cherniss, C. (2010). Emotional intelligence: Toward clarification of a concept. Industrial and Organizational Psychology, 3(2), 110-126.

Goleman, D. (1998). What makes a leader? Harvard Business Review, 76(6), 93-102.

Mayer, J. D., & Salovey, P. (1997). What is emotional intelligence? In P. Salovey & D. Sluyter (Eds.), Emotional Development and Emotional Intelligence: Educational Implications (pp. 3-31). New York: Basic Books.

Van Velsor, E., & Leslie, J. B. (1995). Why executive coaching now? In E. Van Velsor & J. B. Leslie (Eds.), Executive Coaching: An Outcome Study (pp. 1-8). Greensboro, NC: Center for Creative Leadership

Chapter 5 References

Maxwell, J. C. (2011). The 5 levels of leadership: Proven steps to maximize your potential. Center Street.

Molinsky, A. (2013). From global mindset to global skills. Harvard Business Review, 91(11), 139-143.

Porges, S. W. (2011). The polyvagal theory: Neurophysiological foundations of emotions, attachment, communication, and self-regulation. Norton Series on Interpersonal Neurobiology.

www.ingramcontent.com/pod-product-compliance
Lightning Source LLC
Chambersburg PA
CBHW071953210526
45479CB00003B/922